Hummingbirds

Maria Koran

EYEDISCOVER

EYEDISCOVER

Go to **www.eyediscover.com** and enter this book's unique code.

BOOK CODE

AVH73745

EYEDISCOVER brings you optic readalongs that support active learning.

EYEDISCOVER provides enriched content, optimized for tablet use, that supplements and complements this book. EYEDISCOVER books strive to create inspired learning and engage young minds in a total learning experience.

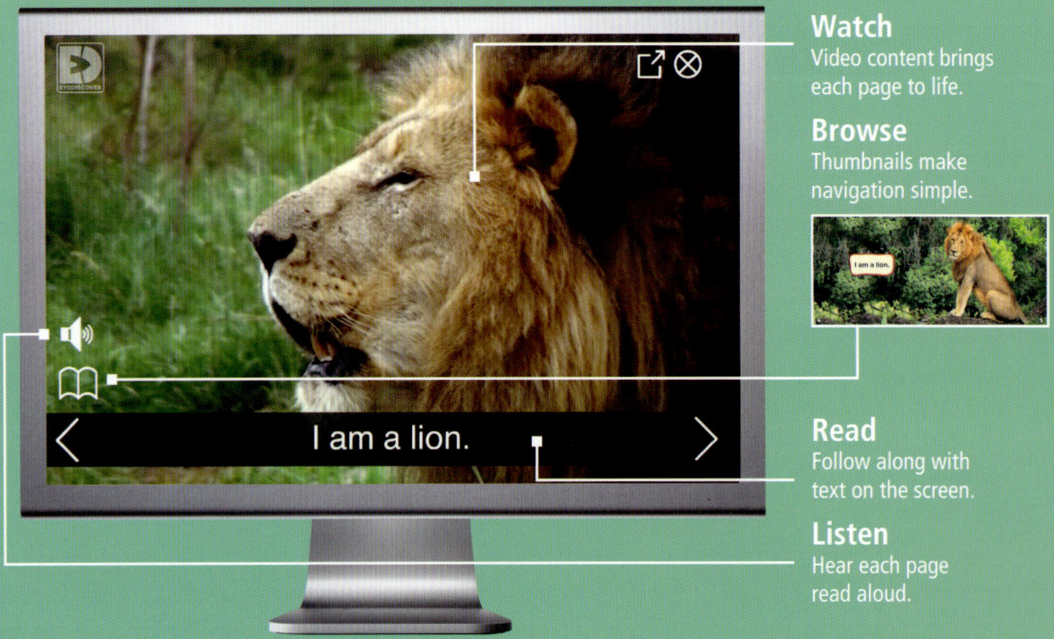

Your EYEDISCOVER Optic Readalongs come alive with...

Audio
Listen to the entire book read aloud.

Video
High resolution videos turn each spread into an optic readalong.

OPTIMIZED FOR

- ✓ TABLETS
- ✓ WHITEBOARDS
- ✓ COMPUTERS
- ✓ AND MUCH MORE!

Published by AV² by Weigl
350 5th Avenue, 59th Floor New York, NY 10118
Website: www.eyediscover.com

Library of Congress Cataloging-in-Publication Data available on request

ISBN 978-1-7911-0760-4 (hardcover)

Printed in Guangzhou, China
1 2 3 4 5 6 7 8 9 0 23 22 21 20 19

072019
121818

Project Coordinator: John Willis
Designer: Mandy Christiansen and Ana María Vidal

Weigl acknowledges Alamy, Getty Images, iStock, and Minden Pictures as the primary image suppliers for this title.

Hummingbirds

In this book, you will learn about

- what they are
- where they live
- what they eat

and much more!

Hummingbirds are colorful birds. Their name comes from the noise their wings make.

Hummingbirds can be very small. The bee hummingbird is the smallest bird.

Hummingbirds
flap their wings
very fast.

Hummingbirds can fly up, down, sideways, and upside down.

Hummingbirds use their eyes to find flowers. They use their long tongues to drink nectar.

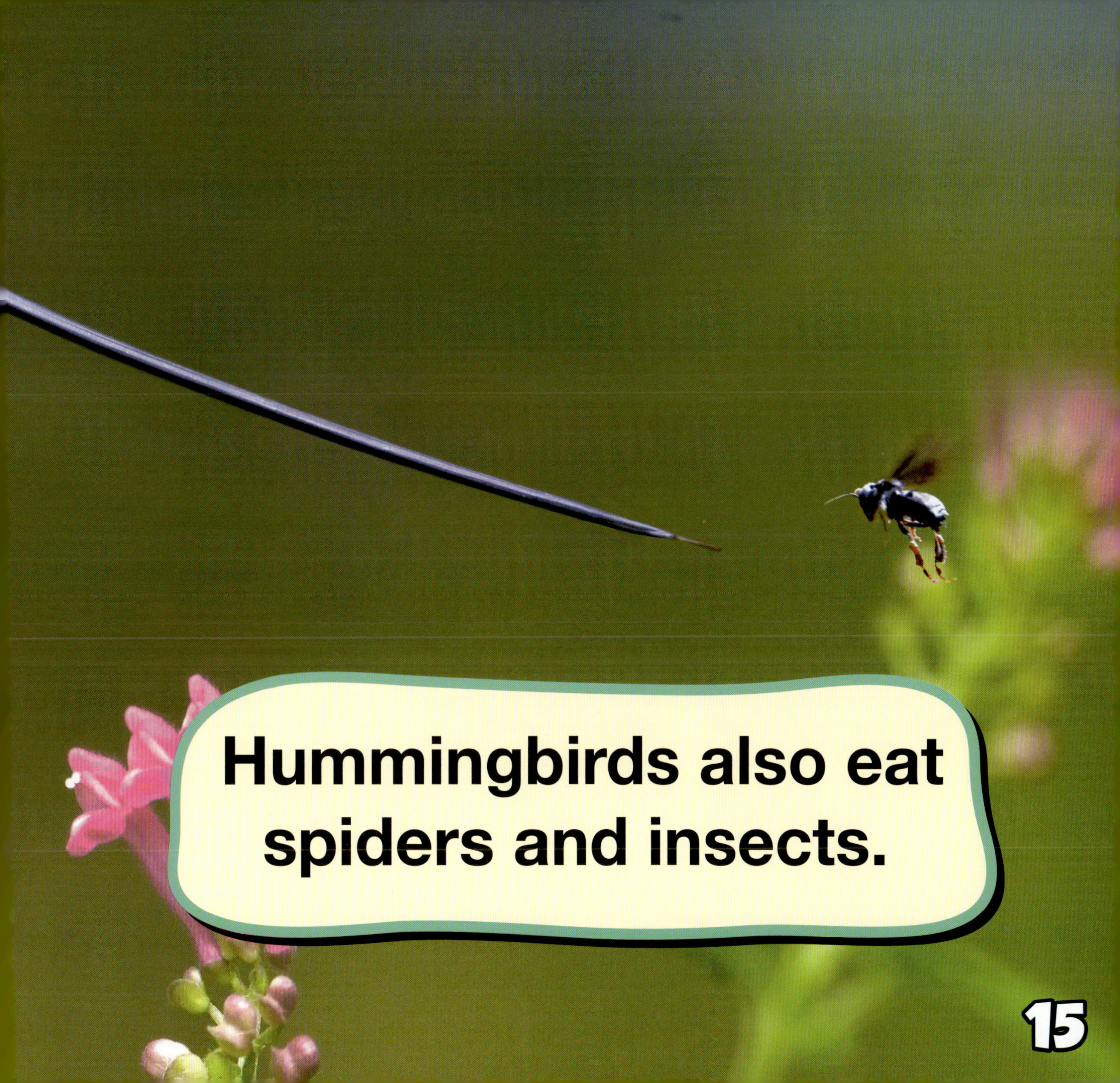

Hummingbirds also eat spiders and insects.

Only 12 kinds of hummingbirds spend summer in North America. They spend winter in warmer places.

Some people feed hummingbirds. It is important to give them the right food.

Many hummingbirds have lost their homes. People can help them by keeping forests safe.

HUMMINGBIRDS BY THE NUMBERS

A resting hummingbird breathes **250 times** each minute.

A **bee hummingbird** weighs **less** than a **penny**.

Bee hummingbirds are about **2.4 inches** long. (6 centimeters)

Some hummingbirds **flap their wings** more than **80 times** each second.

Rufous hummingbirds travel more than **3,000 miles** between Alaska and Mexico each year. (4,800 kilometers)

There are about **320** different kinds of **hummingbirds.**

KEY WORDS

Research has shown that as much as 65 percent of all written material published in English is made up of 300 words. These 300 words cannot be taught using pictures or learned by sounding them out. They must be recognized by sight. This book contains 41 common sight words to help young readers improve their reading fluency and comprehension. This book also teaches young readers several important content words, such as proper nouns. These words are paired with pictures to aid in learning and improve understanding.

Page	Sight Words First Appearance
4	are, comes, from, make, name, the, their
6	be, can, is, small, very
11	and, down, up
12	eyes, find, long, they, to, use
15	also, eat
17	in, kinds, of, only, places
18	food, give, important, it, people, right, some, them
20	by, have, help, homes, many

Page	Content Words First Appearance
4	birds, hummingbirds, wings
6	bee hummingbird
11	sideways, upside down
12	flowers, nectar, tongues
15	insects, spiders
17	North America, summer, winter
20	forests

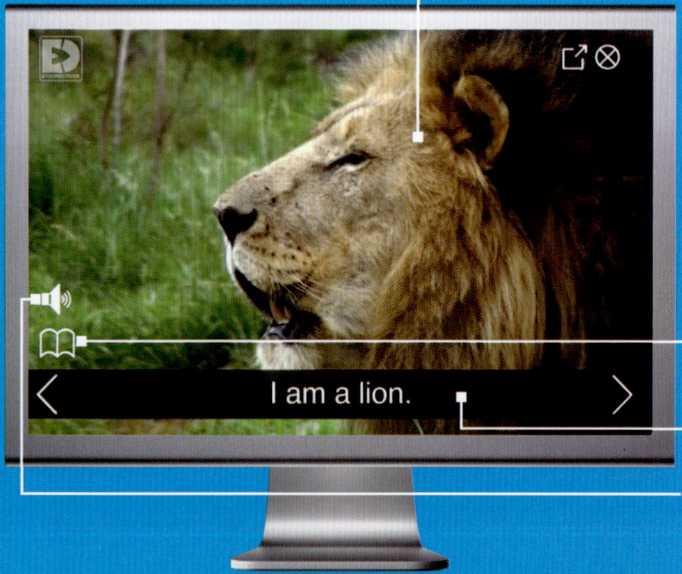

Watch
Video content brings each page to life.

Browse
Thumbnails make navigation simple.

Read
Follow along with text on the screen.

Listen
Hear each page read aloud.

EYEDISCOVER

Go to www.eyediscover.com and enter this book's unique code.

BOOK CODE

AVH73745